The Journey Continues

Janice A. Euell

Copyright © 2024 by Janice A. Euell

All rights reserved. No part of this publication may be reproduced, distributed, or transmitted in any form or by any means, including photocopying, recording, or other electronic or mechanical methods, without the prior written permission of the copyright owner and the publisher, except in the case of brief quotations embodied in critical reviews and certain other noncommercial uses permitted by copyright law. For permission requests, write to the publisher, addressed "Attention: Permissions Coordinator," at the address below.

Books Academy LLC
5900 Balcones Drive Suite 100
Austin, Texas 78731
Hotline: (254) 800-1183

Ordering Information:
Quantity sales. Special discounts are available on quantity purchases by corporations, associations, and others. For details, contact the publisher at the address above.

Printed in the United States of America.

ISBN-13:	Softcover	978-1-964864-02-0
	eBook	978-1-964864-03-7

Library of Congress Control Number: 2024913075

Life is a continuous journey –
Come along for the ride.

I. **International Library of Poetry Selections**
- With love – *Visions of Beauty*
- Without love – *The Road that Never Ends*
- That's when I cry – *Eternal Songs*

I. **Reader's Favorites**
- A. Love is
- B. Dark cloud
- C. Soaring through the clouds
- D. Why is it?
- E That's when I cry

II. **Life's Journeys**

<u>About Life</u>
- What Have You Done?
- Life is
- I have given you
- What made you that way
- I wanna talk about life
- I wrote a poem
- If I could
- If you do nothing

I

- Looking at te sky
- Special event
- Why must I be the glue
- You don't know me
- A mother's love
- Happy anniversary
- You were there
- Your legacies live
- My best friend
- Time
- A blade of grass
- In the meantime
- Just for a minute
- Don't stop the music

Dark Side

- Sad house
- Hurry up and stand still
- Damaged soul
- Conflict
- Cocoon
- Night
- Seasons of rain
- The day the skies cried

- Noise
- They will come to your funeral
- Dark cloud

Humor
- Sunglasses
- Idioms
- Sailing
- Piano blues
- Sexy saxophone
- Hot flashes
- Just chillin'
- My tribulations
- Why women get headaches
- Change of life
- On a cruise
- Comedians
- Frustration

In The Wild
- In the jungle
- The Flowers
- The sssssSnake

Inspiration

- You are a star
- Affirmation of being
- Motherhood
- Crossroads
- In the moment
- Stand up and be counted
- When do you stop?
- I am an artist
- The painter
- Mother
- I can say yes
- It's you
- The power of one
- Wings
- Until you know peace
- What time is tomorrow?
- Looking out of my window
- Freedom is not free
- Smiling
- In the rain
- Coulda been
- When angels cry

Love and Happiness

- Chippin away at mjy love
- In your eyes
- Love is
- Never loved

Romance

- Fire within
- Volcanoooo
- Bed of music
- I had a need
- Without inhibitions

Table Contents

What Have You Done?. 1

Things I Never Wanted 2

The Fire Within 3

 Sunglasses 4

Volcano 6

Life Is 8

I've Given You 9

Bed of Music 10

In the Jungle 12

What Made You That Way? 13

You Are a Star 14

 Affirmation of Being 15

Motherhood 16

Crossroads. 17

Sad House 18

Hurry Up and Stand Still 20

Damaged Soul 22

Conflict 23

My Flight. 24

Idioms	26
Cocoon	28
I Want to Talk About life	29
I wrote a poem	31
If I could	33
If you do nothing	34
In The Mornin'	36
Looking at the sky	37
Night	39
Sailing	41
Seasons Of Rain	42
Soarin' Through The Clouds	44
Special Event	45
Stand Up And Be Counted	46
The Day The Skies Cried	48
That's When I Cry	49
The Noise	51
They Will Come To Your Funeral	52
When Do You Stop?	54
Why Is It?	56
Why Must I Be The Glue?	58
You Don't Know Me	60
I Am An Artist	61
Piano Blues	63

Sexy Saxophone	65
The Painter	66
A Mother's Love	68
Happy Anniversary	70
I Had A Need	72
Mother	74
You Were There	75
Your Legacies Live On	76
Hot Flashes	77
Just Chillin'	79
My Tribulations	80
Why Women Have Headaches	81
Change Of Life	83
Dark Cloud	84
I Can Say Yes	86
It's You	87
The Power Of One	88
Wings	90
Chippin' Away At My Love	91
Friend Ship	93
In Your Eyes	95
Love Is	97
My Best Friend	99
With Love	100

Time	102
Until You Know Peace	104
Blade of Grass	105
I Can't Feel That Rhythm	107
On a Cruise	108
Just a Flower	109
In the Meantime	110
What Time Is Tomorrow	111
The s-s-s-s-s-Snake	112
Looking Out Of My Window	113
The Comedians	114
Freedom is Not Free	115
Without Inhibition	118
Smiling	119
Just for a Minute	120
Never Loved	121
In the rain	122
Coulda Been	123
When Angels Cry	124
Don't Stop the Music	125
Frustration	126

What Have You Done?

I gave you jewelry and other fine things

I gave you money but what did you bring

You were a bum now you look stately
But what have you done for me lately?

I wore the crown and you were my king
You brought what to this party-can you say nothing?
I don't love you but I care for you greatly
Loving you ain't easy 'cause what have you done for me lately

Don't answer that question i know what you've done
Telling every girl you know that they are the one.

They believe you and you go on your way
Just disrespecting them having nothing to say
I know what you say is about so don't debate me
'cause someday you'll ask me what have you done for me lately.

Caio baby

Things I Never Wanted

War
Bias
Prison
Lon lines
Depression
And the list goes on

Diseases
Bad skin
Bungy jumping
Skiing, snowboarding
Jumping from a perfectly good plane
And then calling the queen by her first name

I never wanted to see little children crying
I really never wanted to see anyone dying

All these things of which I have no desire
Happen without my approval.

The Fire Within

On the outside cool, calm and unaffected
On the inside, burning, erotic and hectic
Hidden from family and friends
All the turmoil from the fire within
Unbridled passion trying to be free
All those feelings boiling inside of thee
The fire within is not a campfire
But a wildfire out of control
Destroying every fiber in its path
probably the best emotion you've ever had.

Sunglasses

The power of eyeglasses is tremendous
Able to transform us from mild and meek
To someone or someth8ing that's rather unique.

If you wear eyeglasses, your identity is hidden.
No way to know who you are – strictly forbidden.

A winning smile, a scar on the cheek, the audacity
To believe that those glasses conceal your identity.
Clark Kent looks changed so dramatically
The minute he puts on those eyeglasses.

Wonder woman transforms behind those Foster Grants
Into a super woman but we didn't know that

The FBI and the CIA wear them the minute they step out
They put on dark glasses, so you won't know what they're all about
We should put glasses on angels and cupid
Since that concept assumes that we're that stupid

Wearing those magical glasses are deceiving and
Like an ostrich sticking his head in the sand
No matter if he buries his head, his behind is vulnerable
Just like thinking that those glasses don't make us gullible.

Volcano

Extreme heat, pulsating, rhythmic
Turmoil boiling
Volcano
Waiting for the day that heat
Can be free
Vol can o

Bursting into the air
Exhaling finally
Vol can ooo

Like is a new building waiting
Anxious
Anticipation
Longing for the unexpected

It is a mountain with an upset stomach
Rumbling
Temperature climbing
Slowly rising to the top and then falling
Heaving, inhaling and exhaling

Hear the outside calling
Acid rumbling in its pits, want to get out

Vol can oooooooooooooo!
Erupted
Aaaaaah!

Life Is

A bag of marbles, reds, greens and blues
Clouds clear with all different hues
Like a song with Gladys and one Pip
Like a large boat struggling in the wind with one sail
Like building a house with only one nail

Great happiness yet some sad
A lot of good things and some bad

A smorgasbord of highs and lows
Timeless coated with the beauty of rainbows
Yet despite it all, unpredictability
Life is.

I've Given You

I've given you the best that I can
Talked to you in words that you can understand
Walked with you, given you courage and direction
Loved with you, lavishing you with affection
Now that I've given you the best I have to give
This is the foundation for the life you have to live

The courage you need the inspiration you crave
The strong roots I've given you will take you to your grave
No one will have the ability to strip your power
Because you have endurance that fortifies itself by the hour.

Fly now with confidence, stay away from the ledge
All the skills I've given you are the tools to give you the edge

Bed of Music

Now I lay me down on a bed of music
Listening to my heart as each note flows through it
The thump of the drum echoes in my ear, my desire
Lying on my bed of music sets my soul on fire.

Music touches in places you can't see
Soothing, caressing and massaging me
Like a masseur a professional in his trade
This is no time for the music to fade.

Music is an injection of rhythm that flows through the veins
It takes you to heights that you'll not experience ever again
When you kick back on a bed of music each day
It cleans and replenishes your spirit in a special way.

When you wake with music on your mind and put the notes to work
As you walk, those pains you had no longer hurt.
Music heightens your awareness and covers you
Like standing under a waterfall or feeling the morning dew.

You don't have to have the blues to love the message it has

As you don't have to be a musician to feel the pulsating flow of jazz

When you can understand where music begins and end

And how the notes come together into a spiritual blend

You will have found your bed of music-be still and absorb it

Grab your big, soft pillow, turn up the volume and enjoy it.

In the Jungle

Way out on the Serengeti
Cutting trees with a machete
Watching birds soar magically through the air
There's a cunning cougar in the bush, don't know where.

Tiger up in a tree licking his fur
Looking for his cub but can't find her
The agile cheetah can run so fast
Her incredible speed makes it hard to pass.

The mighty and majestic king of beast
Rules his pride while the lioness provides the feast

These are the scenes that one can see –
In the midst of the wild grows one Acacia tree.

What Made You That Way?

Robbing, stealing killing you went astray
What made you that way
You need love from someone you don't care who
Has anting love done so much damage to you

Living the life of a hermit staying inside
Inadequacies, fear, loneliness you can't hide
Something burning making you scared to be in society
Going from room to room with your anxiety
What made you that way

You gave your all to a cause you believed in
It changed your life in a way more like grieving
But you went on without delay
God made you that way.

You Are a Star

When you gaze at the sky and realize
The beauty and tranquility that he has
Everything there you admire from a far
You on earth wishing on a star.

Night and day you toil to become a success
And sometimes sacrificing your own happiness
Take a closer look at the sky, it's not busy
Marvel in its splendor, it'll make you dizzy.

At night you can't see the clouds, you know they're there
On a clear night, you see bright stars everywhere
Some alone, others forming identifiable shapes
Big dipper, little dipper, they all look great.

Others with wealth, you are wishing with envy
Boy, I would be happy if that could be me
You are great in your own way, you were made that way
You are a star in the heavens,
You are a star, renew your own spirit, God made you that way.

Affirmation of Being

I learned to live while the cameras of my life were rolling

I wasn't born knowing and there were no dress rehearsals

It was on-the-job training and every facet of it was triggered by another

So when did I become a spectator of my life

I won't wallow in regrets or should have(s)

I will celebrate them as I will my life

I don't know how to separate them because I didn't live a portion of my life

I lived it all and every aspect of it – I own

Because it totaled ME

What component could I change and still have great moments

Who would I be

This life is mine and it was meant for me.

Motherhood

Being a mother is the hardest job that I ever had to do
To love your child – to punish you child – to love your child too
To allow your child to love you – to hope your child loves back
Keeping things in line and your lives on track

Being a mother is the hardest job I ever had to do
But I have always wanted what was best for you
And though sometimes you said you couldn't tell
I gave you my best and forever wished you well

I guess that's the nature of our relationship.
Hill and valleys and on with the trip
Down life's lanes of twist and turns
And putting in place what we have learned

For when it's all said and done
We had sad times and fun
And what we remember most
Is that we love each other and will forever remain close.

Crossroads

Have you ever wondered how you missed your crossroad and
Where it was and why didn't you see the turn
Can you imagine how it would have been and – When
What you would do differently and – How
Did others see it or are you the only one that should
And if others saw it— what would they say
And would you listen anyway

Should you don't know anything about the past except that it's gone
Should you remember more than the education you received
Or the lesson of what you believe
Shouldn't you focus on why you are
And isn't going on the part of life that's the
Present slipping into the future
Who you are because of the turns you took
And the choices you made
And if you could do it over again
What would you trade?

Sad House

I brought a sad home yesterday
Though I tried to throw it away
When something made me smile
It disappeared but came back in a little while

It hangs on like a leech.
Is it something that I teach
I wish it would lose oxygen and die
Cause lately all I do is cry

I met with my friends
And I try to drown sad out
But its power dripped my soul
And then I began to shout

I've lost myself or maybe this is me
I feel so empty—what could it be
But trouble and sad
Which makes me damn mad

I brought sad home tonight
I tried to throw it away
Maybe I'll go to sleep
And wake up to a better day.

Hurry Up and Stand Still

I'm somewhere between hurry up
and stand still
Maybe I need a pill
Nooo I don't think so

I have to find that happy medium
Where I can let my mind go
Hope to find a space to dwell
And put on my own show

It has to be a peaceful place
And filled with melodies
Perhaps my own forest
Filled with willow trees

I'll swing from their branches
And embrace the touch of morning dew
Caress the leaves
And sing a song or two

I called to the birds

And request a duo
I'll run with the squirrels
And summon the wind to blow

And I'll put out an extra call to the wild
And will not be afraid
We will gather around
A pond and enjoy what God has made

I will do this one day
When my mind is not far gone
I'll call it my peaceful place
Right here under God's sun.

Damaged Soul

I may not have all the fancy titles or associates that you have

But at mornings light and twilight when I catch a glimpse of my soul

I'm not frightened by what I see

I'm glorified that I had the strength to fight

The demons that crossed my path and whispered loaded promises in my ear

And the wisdom to know that upon the entry of my day –

I was given a mind and heart to use not as a weapon of contempt

Or deceit but as a proponent of peace and goodwill

And I know beyond any reasonable doubt that the likes of you

Will not forever flourish but burn amidst the fires that you set

In an attempt to destroy goodwill and you will become extinct as the dinosaur

And as forgotten as a distant memory of a forgettable floating fog.

Conflict

I am having a thunderstorm on the inside

And a sunny day on the out

Smile at the world and

To myself pout

But I don't have misplaced anger

I direct it where it should go

I say my piece.

And head for the door

To cool my thoughts down

And it won't take long

Just need to vent

Or hear my favorite song.

My Flight

Today I was so sad
I could not help but cry
Tried to maintain control
As I flew thru the sky

A young man sat beside me
And didn't know what to do
I tried to shield him from my cry
But the tears broke thru

He took out his lap top
And he began to read
It filled his time
And to me that was his good deed

Cause I didn't want sympathy
For it would not be good
Cause if I started to talk
I may not stop the tears even if I could

I wanted to say, I'm sorry

But even that caused too much pain
And if ever our paths crossed
I will not do it again.

Idioms

There's a time and place for everything
It's not over 'til the fat lady sings
Can't judge a book by its cover
And the buck stops here

They can continue on but doesn't continue mean that anyway.

Why all the ado about a phrase
When all you need is to just say it.

Our need to be so mysterious
Only makes more of us furious.

Filling sentences with useless disdain
Using those idioms that you must explain.

Having to tell what's meant by a phrase
Defeats its purpose, mad at the one that created it.

Omit the idioms say what you mean

That you won't have to explain anything,

If you do that earnestly you'll see
Idioms should be eliminated from the dictionary.

Cocoon

Wrapped up in a world of confusion,
Waiting my time
My shelter from the world's transgression
Soon will be gone until the next cycle
Trapped in a self-made prison,
Praying to love to be free.

Metamorphosis slowly taking place
New shape forming gradually
Nervously waiting to show the
World my new beauty

I am out on my own.

I Want to Talk About life

With a scholar,
Or with the village idiot
With a child
Or with a homeless guy
I want to talk about life,
Nothing could satisfy me more
Than to know what they think
About politics, about crime,
What would they change?

Anyone ever ask your opinion?
Or do things just happen
And you nod with unquestioning approval?
Don't you want to talk about life?

In every walk of life, there is a person
That has something profound to say,
But who really asks them anything.
We're too busy believing that we have the only answers

I want to talk about life

With a child just learning how to talk
What are their first words, their first sentence
And what was it about?
Food, sleep, something to drink?

Life is much more that what
I think or what you think you know,
It's about a noun,
Persons, places or things,

Or, maybe I don't want to talk about life,
Maybe just living, loving, caring
About myself and my surroundings
Is enough to turn my nouns into adjectives.
Then, I can write about life.

I wrote a poem

In the depth of my soul
Is a story n'er to be told.
I wrote a poem that no one will
E'vr see
'cause it reveals a very private
Part of me

Under the laughter lies a sadness
That sometimes gets me down.
B'neath the smiles, a frown, that
Creeps into my being when'
No one is around

The rain that gently falls from the skies
Are more droplets compared to the
Tears that fall from my eyes.

I wrote a poem praying that emptiness would
Not again visit me and hope to regain
That part of me that is still somewhat sane.

Putting my thoughts on paper
Is a whole lot safer
Then taking my pain to the street
And having a lifeless soul at my feet
So a poem is my salvation.

If I could

If I could stay forever, would I?
Or would I just prefer to die.
Living in a weakened condition,
Is not that a frightening premonition?

If a bird could no longer fly
Would it try?
Or remain on land and let life pass it by?
If I could fly, would i?

Being larger, do you yearn to be thin?
Or am I content in my own skin?
When my stature is small,
Why do I pine to be tall?

Does a bottle want to be a can?
A boy can't wait to be a man.
When your looks don't change even when you try
Can only be achieved if you're a butterfly.

Resentment to contentment? I can.

If you do nothing

A flat tire in the morning.
Leaky faucet that didn't leak the night before.
Another ache, another pain,
All of these things happen,
If you do nothing.

If you do nothing but rise
A new problem will materialize,
If you mind your own business
Life brings you grief and
Complications arrive unsolicited at your door.

Power outages
Refrigerator won't freeze – it did the night before.
Washer stopped washing,
Dryer stopped drying,
And you did absolutely nothing to make things happen.

No need to create problems for yourself
They come freely and unprovoked.
The sun will rise and set,

The wind will blow, flowers will bloom,
If you do nothing.

Crime and violence remain on your street.
Politicians that don't consider your issues,
The wrong person gets in office.
The world does not become a better place,
If you do nothing at all.

In The Mornin'

Looking at my situation tonight, it looks pretty sad.
Whoever heard of any person's life being so bad?

Nothing going right, things comin' up without warning
But my mother told me,
"things always look better in the mornin'"

Well, mama, God love her, I've tried to believe
In her wisdom, and I've tried to achieve.

Workin' hard every day trying to do the right thing
Wanna get up in the morning' and hear the birds sing.

But life tonight is pretty much the same as yesterday
Getting up in the mornin' is just God's way

Of telling us to have faith, there's a new day dawnin'
And truthfully, with all my trials,
There's nothing like getting up in the mornin'.

Looking at the sky

Looking at the sky through the trees,
Your view is sometimes obstructed by the leaves
In the winter, you see the foliage disappear
Then the blue sky seems so beautiful and clear.

When the ice clings to the tree branches,
The sky may be grayer, but the ice enhances.
It's beauty its charm and grace
Looking at the sky even then brings a smile to my face.

The sky is constantly changing, different hues, shapes,
And sizes.
The reds, oranges and blues and many other
Panoramic surprises.
Unlike the trees, the sky give no indication season
If gives us magnificence and light shows all year
For no real reason.

Blue sky, white clouds, bright sunshine and clear.
Gray skies, gray clouds bring rain during the year
Violent dark clouds could bring tornadoes and storms

But our clouds, delight, excite and forewarn.

Clouds help us predict the weather, at least we try,
You see, you can learn so much just looking at the sky.

Night

Hark! The night falls
Rainbows over the land disappear
Haunting eyes stare down from the sky
No color, everything is black or white
Lo' the mystery of the night.

The night casts shadows
Reflection of the soul
That hideth behind eyes of glistening coal
Cryin' out for salvation
In a story yet to be told.

The night is deceiving
Things unthreatening during the day
Take on different shapes in the night
Chillin' your inner psychic,
Making you believe things your eyes do no see.

Yet the night has its intrigue

Makes you see things in a different light
It presents more challenges.
The beauty of the day doth not reappear,
When you are no longer here.

Sailing

Such a panoramic view
Blue sky, not a cloud
Waves gently massage
The rocky shore

The motion of the ride
Stretching out to touch land, then receding
Sails in different colors
Boats, all sizes
Yachts, speed boats

Ocean rising up and then exhaling
Relaxes your mind and spirit.
The water takes you to another special place.
Makes your soul feel relief to be
In unison with the elements

Sailing, riding the waves like a bronco.
When you're feeling this good
You want to float.
Now, all you need is a boat.

Seasons Of Rain

Winter, the rain comes, cold air turns it to ice.
Nothing you wear every seems to suffice,
When the cold winds blow, there's no doubt
That any sensible person will want to go out.

Flower buds peeking out in the morning dew
Opening their arms to welcome you
A light soft sprinkle starts life in the spring
Getting caught in the rain is a delightful thing.

Summer raindrops, warm and cool
A walk in the rain, no umbrella, just the winter and you.

Thunderstorms are raindrops gone mad
Some of the worse we've ever had
Tornadoes, flooding and hurricanes
So vicious they gave them all names.

The rhythm of the raindrops signal it's fall.
Pumpkins. The rain brings a great harvest for all.
The seasons of rain come and go no matter the season,
It can bring joy or pain for no obvious reasons.

Soarin' Through The Clouds

Soarin' through the clouds
Many places I can see
Old and new, big and small
My spirit runs free.

I fly high on days when exhilaration I feel
And low at times when frustration is real.

In the clouds, soft
Fluffy ones, white and blue
Cleanse your soul
Your worries subdued.

A trip in the clouds high up above
Would not be possible without God's love.

Soar through the clouds with an open mind
Peace in the clouds you shall find.

Special Event

As a seed, I lay dormant inside
Waiting for my time to arrive.
At the mercy of someone else to decide.

Waiting patiently for the ultimate surprise
Of being able to open my eyes
And for the world to hear my cries.

No one knows what I have to endure, it's not right
Being in limited space, wet with no light.
Angry, but can't put up a fight.

I struggle and struggle trying to get out.
No one knows what my unrest is about.
It's just contractions, no doubt.

To waiting hands, I am delivered.
To another prison, just bigger,
Special event. Heaven sent or hell bent.

Stand Up And Be Counted

You, yes you, get off your lazy behind
Open up a newspaper and see what you can find.
Turn on the radio and listen to the news
Call them up and give them your views.

Get the remote and turn the television on to see
If there's a situation brewing in the Middle East.
It's time for you to stop letting everyone else do things for you.
Check out what's happening and see what you can do.

Stand up and be counted, be proud and active
Find a situation in which you can be proactive
Many lives were lost for you to have certain rights
For some things, you have to take a stand and fight.

But fighting each other is not one of the choices
There are other ways for others to hear our voices
Stand up and be counted, exercise your right to vote
If you're not paying attention, you may miss the boat.

Teach your children to care about the land,
When you see a child in despair, lend a helping hand.
If you don't take a position on what's right and wrong,
You'll continue to complain, singing that same old song.

Your participation is solicited and appreciated, indeed,
To make decisions about our country's many needs.
So stand up and be counted or be seated and settle for less
Until you become a part of the solution, you really can't
Expect the best.

The Day The Skies Cried

The pain of waking, without you.
Heart aching
Sadness,
Tears in my eyes
Was the day the skies cried.

The unfilled desires
Hurt from a love gone bad
The love of your life died
On that day, the skies cried.

Heartbreak, love forever gone
Been here an now you're alone
The rains come to hide the tears
That fall from your eyes
Every time the skies cry.

That's When I Cry

When love is lost and can't be found
Children are hurting, no parents around,
A beggar with no food to eat
A lonely soul with no shoes on his feet,
That's when I cry.

Hearing the wind howling on a cold winter night
Or a baby crying in its room from fright,
A mama whose child lost his life to crime
A father searching for a child he can't find,
That's when I cry.

When war turns our neighborhoods into debris
Refugees fighting 'cause they want to be free
Tornadoes destroying everything in their way
Floods and hurricanes, the devastation, the decay,
That's when I cry.

A rose delivered because someone really loves me

Thoughtful notes, kind gestures, a heart full of glee,
Friends, family, bring flowers while you are alive
Waiting arms to caress me as I arrive,
That's also when I cry.

The Noise

My inner spirit is quiet.
I hear the thoughts in my mind.
Thoughts about living
Those regrets about dying
I pray for the noise

With the noise I put
Unpleasantries to rest.
I don't have to listen to my inner pain.
I bring in the noise but
Tribulations come again.

Horrible things I did, deceit, lies
Neglect and crimes
Though I'm not trying, sad memories
Take over my inner being.

I hear my noise but for you, it takes a new slant
You want to forget life's miseries, but you can't
Some things in your past you want to avoid
By keeping the volume turned up on the noise.

They Will Come To Your Funeral

It's sorta odd and somewhat strange
Many people know your name,
Your friend they claim to be
Your face they seldom see,
But they will come to your funeral.

A card, some flowers while you live
None of these will they give.
Kind words, a gift, a shoulder on which to cry,
Fail to show they love you until you die.

Sadness, problems, disappointments, deeply blue,
No one to listen or care about you.
Sit alone and ponder, wonder why
Friends don't like you til you expire.
And, they will come to your funeral.

They wouldn't come to visit not for a minute.

Is the world a better place without you in it?
Are they crying at your funeral because you're gone?
Or sad 'cause it took you so long?
No mat'r, they will come to your funeral.

When Do You Stop?

Violence, hatred, and many lives wasted
All because of you
'cause you can't face it
What are going to do?

When do you stop being the game
Being pursued by the hunters
Drug users and dealers know the hunters by name
And they'll know your name when you go under.

Crime and chaos have become a part of your life
For more than twenty years
You've abandoned your children and your wife
Leaving them at home in tears.

A job to you is a foreign, unimaginable thing
An enigma if you will
You never gave your wife a wedding ring
You know all of this and still.....

You don't stop. You're outta control
Your life is a terrible mess
Can't help you, but save your child's soul
Start anew – just confess.

'cause if you can't stop
Life passes you by
Just when you decide to stop
May be your time to die.

Why Is It?

That the other line always seems to move faster?
Or the grass on the other side always looks greener?
Why do some lives end in disaster?
And no matter how nice you are, the meaner
Just keep getting meaner.

That you love someone, and they love someone other than you?
That one foot is bigger than the other?
Can't seem to find a friend that is really true.

An act of kindness doesn't come from a sister or brother?
Sometimes you wonder, indeed you do.
Why the stars hang precariously in the sky.

Why so people think there's a man in the moon? That's not true.
Sometimes the wondering makes me want to cry.

I ask myself why is it? And no answer comes right away.
I ask others and they have to speculate.

Instead of continuing to ask why, I put my queries aside,
Or just plain disregard it, 'cause the answers really can wait.

Why Must I Be The Glue?

Why must I be the glue that holds everything together
Consoling everyone until their lives get better?

When tears fall from their faces like rain.
When their faces are gently contorted from pain.

When things go wrong and they don't know what to do,
I hear the call, dear Lord, to provide the glue.

Why must I be the glue that binds a family in love?
In this a gift of compassion, an inspiration from above?

When a child somewhere cries in pain from abuse.
Must be the times I want to sleep, but there's no use.

The empathetic side of me feels the pain and sorrow,
Of those long forgotten with no hopes for tomorrow.

When I see someone hungry with nothing to eat.
Or a person walking without shoes on their feet.

I feel drawn to find a way for their lives to renew
There I go again, Lord, wanting to be the glue.

God has apparently seen fit to bestow on me this
Precious gift.
To provide hope for those needing an inspirational lift.

Who am I to question or otherwise complain about what
I must do?
I guess, dear Lord, the answer is because you want me to.

You Don't Know Me

We have never been further apart.
Though I've wanted to be closer with all my heart.
I call but you're too busy or slow to react.
For some reason, you just can't call back,

Our lives have been intertwined for many years.
Yet you know nothing of my pleasures or fears,
When asked if I prefer a movie or a play
You wouldn't have much to say,
Because you really don't know me.

Strangers in your life about whom you know more.
I may be the stranger as I walk through your door.
My likes, favorites, or my whimsical toy
You don't know what things bring me joy.

Do I like to travel, or prefer to stay at home?
Is fear a factor when I'm alone?
Am I handling my afflictions well?
There's no way for you to tell
Why? Because you don't know me.

I Am An Artist

I am an artist with an inherent ability
To paint what I do or do not see.

The color of the sky can be what I want it to be
I can illustrate the calmness of an ocean or sea.

A person's face can be happy, sad or full of dismay.
A day can be cloudy with everything else gray.

From my palette I can create exactly what I feel.
A scene can be fantasy or it can be real.

I can paint diplomats or a clown just joking,
But I can't paint anything when my heart is broken.

I can create a vision for all to see,
But I can't paint a love that lasts for eternity.

I can put on canvas my innermost thoughts and desires,
Which could be cold as the north or as passionate as fire.

I admire scenes and places of beauty, so I work my hardest
Using my palette to turn reality to dreams, because I am
An artist.

Piano Blues

Since I was a little girl, I loved the piano,
Where I got that feeling I really don't know

My mama didn't play, neither did my Dad,
But playing the piano is the fondest dream I ever had.

Those pearly whites and blacks look so intimidating,
Trying to decipher which key plays what tune - so frustrating!

I'm gonna sit on that bench put my fingers in place,
No F key or clef is gonna put a frown on my face.

Admittedly, my heart's racing, my hands shaking a bit,
No more nervous about that first note could I get.

It takes the left and the right sides of my brain,
To play an intelligible tune that you can call by name.

I practice until my fingertips turned blue,
And twinkle, twinkle little star was the best I could do.

So I sat on that bench, posture upright.
Fingers in place, but I was still so uptight.

I'll conquer my piano blues by just whistling a tune.
And promise to get back to the ivory very soon

When perspiration no longer hangs from my brow,
I'll learn to play someday, but not now.

Sexy Saxophone

Sassy notes, so soothing
Suddenly you feel like moving
Rocking gently from side to side
Emotions surfacing. You can't hide
That's the rhythm of the sexy saxophone.

It's perfect body. Such pizzazz.
Falling prey to the smooth jazz,
That emanates from its soul
Resulting in a sound so bold.
A romantic interlude.

The sound takes you to a new place
The look of contentment spreads over your face
Doesn't matter if it's music or song
Nothing can really go wrong
When you listen to the melodies from the saxophone

Sadness, problems all disappear
When sex sounds are all you hear.
Pleasure. Listening in a crowd or alone.
Nothing matches the soul stirring saxophone.

The Painter

The Painter needed a world with a lot color in it
His list of ideas for beauty seem infinite.
He looked at the sky and decided just blue would not do
So he chose a variety of colors and hues.

"Trees, what shall I do with them?" he said.
"Perhaps, a selection of green, yellow, brown and red."
"But, wait," He said, "something is missing to me.
I shall also paint rivers, oceans and seas.

Everything seemed too flat for the world to be right
He needed majestic mountains rising to new heights,
To complete His idea of the perfect painting. He cried,
"There must be people here to see this and admire.

He stood and looked at this wondrous thing He had done
This perfect painting could not be duplicated by anyone
It was a masterpiece no other copies to be made
Everlasting beauty created that will never ever fade.

When He painted the day, He painted the night

But still something wasn't exactly right.
The day was full of beauty to appease the eye,
Which all disappeared when the evening drew nigh.

He decorated the night sky with stars and the moon
To light our way
Until we open our eyes to the dawn of a new day
Thanks to the Painter for creating such beauty
To protect it and take of it is now our duty.

A Mother's Love

Like a flower waking with the morning dew
Basking in the warmth of the sun, its spirit to renew
Like watching on a clear night the stars above
Nothing surpasses the tenderness of a mother's love

Chastising you, she has your best interest at heart
She wants life's treasures for you from the start.

Asking you to do your chores, she's training
Telling you to wear rain gear when it's raining.

She is the doctor wanting your body and mind to heal
From any stress or strain you might feel.

As a psychiatrist, she listens intently to your woes
Like a general, she strategizes how to defeat your foes.

In a carpool, she is the driver to your track and field meet
As a chef, she prepares scrumptious meals for you to eat.

Her compassion and devotion run deep like still water
Making no difference between her son and daughter.

When you're down, she's there no cushion your fall
She's always available whenever you call.

She brings happiness and peace to your life like a dove
Nothing equals the depth of a mother's love.

Happy Anniversary

With this ring, I thee wed,
On our wedding day is what we said.

Sacrifice and compromise all of our lives
Having children with an unpredictable wife.

Ove the years we have struggled to make ends meet
But through it all, we overcame every defeat.

In our years together, we have had great and bad times
Yet, you're the best husband I could ever find.

We have laughed together and yes we have cried
We have lived through the truth and yes a few lies.

No matter what the consequence, we have survived
'cause we have love and compassion in our lives

Some say you deserve a medal and maybe you do
To live with me so long and perhaps that's true.

You helped me walk when I only thought I could crawl
And you've always been there to break my fall.

For this occasion, I must tell you what I feel and I truly mean it
To have, to hold, is our fate for all eternity.

I Had A Need

I felt for the pillow
Where you laid your head,
My mind played the words
That you once said,
I had a need this mornin'
And I didn't know what to do.

The pain of your leaving
Was still fresh in my heart
I never dreamed that
Someday we'd part.

You left an emptiness in
A deep, dark place.
Tho' you're gone, every
Minute I see you face.

Where you've gone you
Will never return
Leaving my heart to fore'er yearn
For the love we once had

My spirit will never heal because your
Leaving has hurt me so bad.

I had a need that only your touch could fulfill
Many have tried, but no one ever will
I had a need this mornin' and I didn't know what to do
'cause I can't walk, touch or feel without you.

Mother

She was mysterious,
Unpredictable, fun
And a little crazy.

A lady of leisure,
Confident and carefree.
Special because she
Gave birth to me.

Caring, forgivin', calculating.
Decisive and demanding
An accomplished chef, you'd
Love anything she had her hand in.

In her, no comparison,
There will never,
Be another
Certain mysteries about her unraveled
As I became a mother.

You Were There

When I took my first breath
Took my first step.
As I started my first grade
The mistakes I made.
You were there when I had my first fight
I tried to run away with all of my might.
A big step in my life
When I became a new wife.
When I had my first child
You greeted him with an adoring smile.
And my second blessed event
A girl who was also heaven sent.
You were there when losses in my life lead to despair
I was there when gray replaced the black in your hair.
For every special and blessed event, Dad, you've been
A friend so true.
And now, it's my chance to be there for you.

Your Legacies Live On

It is in your memory
That these lines are written
Neither of you we can think about forgetting
Your sons and daughters will thrive in love
Knowing that you rest peacefully above
In your light, our accomplishments shine
Your guidance and leadership were so divine.
We are happy that to you we were born
Because of you, your legacies live on.
All that we are or ever hope to be
Was because you set our minds free.
When we look at each other, your faces we see
We love and praise you as your legacies live on for eternity.
You were here but now you are gone from our sight
But your legacies live on, we try to do what's right.

Dedicated to the memory of my parents
Bessie Swinnie Crowder
William Martin Crowder

Hot Flashes

Hot flashes have a very bad reputation
Is there any truth in it,
You're okay now but
In just one minute
Sweating
Running for the door
Opening the windows.

Keep a handkerchief in hand,
Not thinking about a man,
Trying to cool and feel cool.
Instead you look more like a fool.

People in heavy coats, buttoned to the neck
You're the only one sweating
Whole body soaking wet.

This had to be a punishment
Manufactured by Satan
No one else could conjour
Up such a hellish situation

How to identify a person with those hot flashes?
While you are standing still, they're the
Ones running fast past you
Not necessarily doing it with flair
Just rushing to the window to get some fresh air.

Just Chillin'

Sipping tea, swinging in the breeze
Just watching the wind gently caress the oak tree leaves
Got a job to do, but sure ain't willin'
'Cause I'm much happier when I'm just chillin'

Bring on the lemonade while I'm rocking
Don't want to hear no one knocking
Ice cold drink to massage my mind
This is the best life a lazy mind can find.

Don't want no problems, no family or friends
Who can't understand the state of mind I'm in
When I'm chillin', I reject the noise
Made by men, women, little girls or boys.

Just me. Laid back, care and worry free
problems bother me
If you can't imagine just how I'm feelin'
Then you need to find out what it feels like to be just chillin'.

My Tribulations

My back is aching so is my knee
The bottoms of my feet are as sore as can be.

I've walked a mile in shoes that are two sizes too small
Must have lost my mind shopping for them at the mall.

My eyes are blurred, sometimes can't see a lick
When darkness comes, glasses too thick.

My throat is dry, my back is starting to itch
Either I'm catching a cold, getting old, I don't know which.

You told me something yesterday, now I can't recall
Was it important? Don't know. Can't tell you at all.

My tribulations aren't as paramount as they seem.
'Cause I work up this morning and it was all a dream.

Why Women Have Headaches

They live with
Make love to them
Fight over trivia
With Men

Because men can't find their socks
Lose their keys
Can't remember to get a loaf of broad
From the corner store
On their way home.

No, women don't know
What you want to eat.
Have to live with you and your
Smelly feet
And because you snore.

Women have headaches because
You won't ask for directions
Can't remember birthdays
Anniversaries and you

Don't know your children's first names.

A man's "where is my" syndrome
Can't find a thing in your own home.
What you're looking for is right in your face
One would think you rented the place
Your skull is looking for a tenant.

Nevertheless, God loves you
And
So do women!

Change Of Life

You got a bad attitude
You're rude
And loud.

Grow up make a new life for yourself now
Do you know how?
Make success a vow.

Stop blaming others for your sad mistakes
All that crying is a serious fake
Change your life before it's too late.

Realize you can do anything if you try
Make an effort.
Questioning you seems like you're on trial
No, its just to get you out of self-denial
Set goals, achieve, experience life for a while.

This is your change of life request for you to do your best
Don't settle for less.

Changing your life is your destiny
Change it for you and not for me.

Dark Cloud

There's a dark cloud hanging over your head
You should be happy but you're sad instead
There's a dark cloud hanging over your head.

There's a strange cloud enveloping your head
Change your life before you end up dead.
There is no future in death.

A dark cloud has you constantly and fearfully on the run
Miserable, when should be having fun
That's a sad situation, ain't it?

The dark cloud won't leave you alone.
Childhood sadness and now you're grown.
Ain't it time to live now?

You lurk in the alley day by day like a rat
Robbing, stealing, set back after set back.
This is not a bad life, jut live it.

That dark cloud can be removed and it's not hard.
You just need to get a little closer to God.
Turn the black cloud into one with silver thing.

Without God you can do nothing positive that is
Look for faith and happiness life gives
Fully appreciate this precious gift.

Yeah, lift that black cloud and bring yourself joy
Contentment and peace in life you can enjoy
The choice is yours

That dark cloud hovering up above
Can be changed with just a little love.
Love is not painful

I Can Say Yes

I can say yes because I am strong
Because I know what's right or wrong

Peer pressure they claim can destroy me
My parents taught me to love myself, how can that be?

I can't believe the hype I hear on the street
I'm told to dance to a different beat.

I can yes when there's a positive situation
To avoid possible incarceration.

Behind bars, I can't plan or dream
Isolation is as tough as it seems

I don't listen to you, what do you know?
You're burning your brains out on that stuff called blow.

I can say yes to a life without crime
Because the name on success is mine.

It's You

I am a very special person with very special needs
I require the best, and certainly want to succeed.
I have an inspiration that's tried and true
And that inspiration, I believe, it's you.

It's you, I'm certain, you are always around
To listen when my heart is on the rebound.
When getting up in the morning is a chore for me
It's the memory of your smile that sets my soul free.

Yes, it's true, it's really you
Who lights the embers of my being
Who looks beyond what others are seeing

I am a happy person, full of excitement and glee
Concentrating on those things that satisfy me.
I'm wild, kinds silly and sometimes crazy
And yeah, I'm interesting, intriguing and definitely lazy.

But when I'm my best and everything else is tried and true.
I attribute my happiness to me and to you.

The Power Of One

It's really amazing what can be done
In life these days by the power of one.

Seeing litter on the street is really tough
When you see a piece of trash, pick it up.

If one person agrees to be racially aware
No prejudice or animosity would be in the air.

As a volunteer, you can accomplish a lot
When you realize all the talent you've got.

If we care about the earth, appreciate fresh air
Each person must be prepared to do their share.

Don't point your finger accusingly a the other guy
You are the one who must tell your children why.

You neglected the earth and everything in it
You smoked and drank no remembering any of it.

Careless and confused, you've hurt everyone in your path
Just how long do you think this destruction can last?

Sure you're just one person but so is everyone
It's exhilarating the difference we make as the power of one.

Wings

On the wings of dissension
Are situations too critical to mention.
The wings of desperation and despair
Are laden with those that just don't care.

Outstretched arms give the appearance of wings
But illusions are very disconcerting things.
Wings are for soaring high up above
White clouds, majestic mountains, expressions of love.

With wings you could fly from fantasy to reality
Visiting every place in the world you've wanted to see.
Clipped wings injured one day in a storm and
Making you land bound for a while without warning.

To learn to survive on land when your domain is the sky
Makes life seem unfair and you wonder why.
Imagine your wings unfolded for flight
Taking you to new places soaring to new heights.

Imagine your ambition and goals as your wings
You will be able to accomplish some incredible things.

Chippin' Away At My Love

Broken promises
Blatant lies
Inconsistent behavior
Betrayal
You have started to chip away at my love.

Love started true.
Passionate
Trusting
Caring
Two hearts merged into one.

Years pass
Love taken for granted
It takes my love down another peg
Because you didn't do something you said

I loved you when our love was forbidden
When we had to keep our love hidden
I sacrificed some things quite personal
To have your love but worst of all

The fantasy faded, feelings started to erode.

Romantically, we are not where we used to be
Because you have destroyed that faith you see
Ev'ry lie, or act of deceit brings wrath from below
B'cause you have chipped away at my love
And shipped it into an unrecognizable emotion.

Friend Ship

Called so because some friends
Pass like ships in the night
Here today and gone tonight.

Friend ship because everyone
On board is familiar
Consoling and close, real close?

Must be a good thing to have
A friend ship as we struggle
To call each other friend

Friend ship because of the heavy
Load that being a friend
Actually is.
Took much is taken for granted
As a friend.

To be a friend is not to be a pest
A reporter, always inquiring
Being there does not mean

Everyday in the way.

Friend and ship were joined together
To support each other - when needed
To console as required
To meet when desired.
Friendship a vessel to be loved and admired.

In Your Eyes

Beauty, reflection, confidence
Surprise
All this I see in your eyes.

Mystery, suspense, intrigue
Deep down it lies
In the area, the crevices behind your eyes.

Love, admiration, sadness and
Grief
Tear falling from your eyes
Bring some relief
From the pain you feel deep inside
That you can't hide because of your eyes.

In your eyes, all emotions abide
No matter how hard you try to hide
Behind the blindfolds or dark sunglasses
The eyes watch carefully as your life passes.

Happiness, contentment, full of life and
Glee
A gleam in your eyes for the world to see
Broken promises you did not realize
Can't always be detected in your eyes.

Love Is

Love is a warm fire in your fireplace.
It's embers light up the smile on your face
Love is a midnight walk on the beach
Looking at the stars you can't reach.

Built on sacrifice and deep emotion
For a special person deserving your devotion
It's being there for that special someone
In sickness, in health and while having fun.

Is patient, understanding and compromise
With plenty of rewards for those that try.
Love is holding each other 'til the sun rises
Looking passionately into each other's eyes.

It is going through all of the ups and downs
Wanting to be together through joy and frowns
Love is like a river overflowing its bank
Sometime wanting to give up, but you can't

Love is a rainbow. There just for you

To enjoy, to dream and when you're through
Go arm in arm, play in the rain
Because love is all of these things, but
With love there is no pain.

When heartache outweigh love, it's time to get out
Because someone doesn't understand what love is about

Love is a lot of things. The list is infinite.
But life is not worth living without you in it.

My Best Friend

Who is that person so honorable and great
So trustworthy and dependable and never late?
The one who always stands by me in thick or thin.
Who rescues me no matter what situation I'm in?
My best friend

My personal issues are discussed with the utmost care
When I am happy or sad, you're always there.
It doesn't matter to you if I'm on the bottom or the top
If I try a new project you don't care if it's a flop.
You're my best friend

A peculiar person like me needs a person like you
Though we don't say I love you everyday we know it's true
On the road to adventure you're the best driver
During a nature hike you're always the survivor.

Since I met you, I've stop searching for a confident
Because you're the person that I surely want
To share my good times or when my heart's on the mend
I can find no other person on whom I can depend.
I guess that's why you're my best friend.

With Love

I think of the rain
Tapping gently on my window pane.

I'm reminded how special you make me feel
And how comforting it is to know your love is real.

I smile because of how good I feel inside
And when I can't be with your sometimes, how I've cried

You mean so much to me, as I have told you
Many times before,
But when I thought of you today, I wanted to tell you
Once more.

I love you and you are a special part of me
Because when I think of you, it makes me more than happy

I think of how crazy and silly you sometimes are
And how I am comforted to know that you're never far.

In other words, what I am trying to say
Is that you have impacted my life in a satisfying way.

That I hope our relationship will endure all tests of time
Finding me in your arms and you in mine.

I love you.

Time

It's a time and place for everything
A time to dance, protest, a time to sing
There's a time to stand up instead of against the wall
Better to be known for something than nothing at all

Time changes, it moves up and down
And frustrating as that is, it comes back around
We;ve got time out, time being, and time on the tick tock
Wasting time, time after time and a time clock

It's a lot about time that we just don't get
Especially when time anagrammed is emit
Time decides who stays young and who gets old, that's a fact
Time turns your smooth face into a road map

We say we don't have time to do that or this
Have a good time for the moment-don't worry what you miss
You can't save time, it doesn't collect any interest or dividend

When time runs through a sieve, look at the mess you're in

We say we don't have time but that's just not true
Until time runs out what else you gonna do
Don't let time take over and become your master
Because the end of time seems to come much faster

Take your time.

Until You Know Peace

You can't know true satisfaction
Judging others' reaction
You won't be able to find a true release
Until you know peace.

Peace is a state of mind
Doesn't matter if you're deaf, crazy or blind
It's the feeling you have deep within
That's where true peace really begins

A period of tranquility that says everything's alright
You can relax dream, night after night
Except you feel that calmness also during the day
Until you know peace you won't understand what I have to say

Blade of Grass

A mountain is mighty and majestic and still

Vegetation finds its way around it against its will

All the trees and flowers growing so fast

In the midst of all of that grows a blade of grass.

On a craggy hill jutting out everywhere

Look closely you find a blade of grass there

Between a rock and the proverbial hard place

It grows in spite of the odds, persevering unafraid

Grass seed planted in a bed of sand virtually on its own

Then one day the blades join together to form your lawn

Admire the strength, the courage and endurance

That single blade of grass should give you assurance

To move forward with confidence no matter the consequence

You'll look back with satisfaction at the valuable time you spent

Be a glade of grass, endure, conquer the mountain

Be a football field

A manicured lawn

It all started with a single blade of grass.

I Can't Feel That Rhythm

With eerie beat of defeat
The melodies from a harp
Undulating from the hum of the drums
But when it brings pain into my life
I can't feel that rhythm

Happiness dancing on a string
Hypnotic in its motion
Something soothing like watching the waves
Inhale and exhale in the ocean
When you purposely disappoint me, I can't feel that rhythm

I'm neither desperate or lonely
Thinking of you only
Not now or ever are you the only one
Especially when being around you is no longer fun

I can't consider your comments undeserved criticism
'cause you spend too much time trying to interfere with my rhythm

On a Cruise

Goin' on a cruise is a vacation you chose
You're on the water where the spirit of god flows
Flags waving in the warm tropical air
You got bills back at home, for now you don't care.

Enjoy the wine, friends and songs
'cause you'll be back in the race before long
Swim, play games and consume exotic food
If you could stay there you would.

Sunshine, brick and light and that's not all
Dress up, look great sit at the captain's table
This is the kind of fun everyone can use
A unique experience while you've on a cruise

Just a Flower

From a seed
Roots, a stem
A bud opens its eyes
It blooms faster than you realize.

It's beauty unquestionable
So many colors and hues
Shapes, sizes and varieties
More than you can count.

Fragrances so many choices
Occaions, unlimited
Decorations, weddings
A valentine, be mine.

Know that it has such great power
All of this you find in beautiful flower

In the Meantime

The future you have to plan it
Tomorrow not here yet
Mysterious things you can't understand it
Memories some to remember others to forget
But in the meantime…

You're gonna buy that new car
Invest in luxurious house
I wanna go to the movie, it might be bizarre
You wish folds would just tell it like it is
But in the meantime…

Hopes, dreams, aspirations put on hold
'cause you're planning instead of doing it
Don't wait 'til the reality of life turns cold
In the meantime, as you wait, you might just forget.

What Time Is Tomorrow

Tomorrow is not promised
Don't put off tomorrow
What you an do today
Tomorrow will be another day
What else about tomorrow can one say
Actually, what times is it tomorrow anyway

Yesterday we know 'cause that time is ago
Today, we're living it and it never goes slow
We plan for tomorrow but it never arrives
So we should plan for our next today.

We speak of tomorrow and rename it at twelve-o-milli-second
At that time today becomes yesterday and a new today comes.
We talk about tomorrow but in reality
It's a topic for a discussion but a day you never see
So what time is tomorrow who knows who cares
Plan for your todays if you want to get somewhere.

The s-s-s-s-s-Snake

This animal has been living in history since the beginning
Supposedly it was the cause of Eve and Adam sinning
It shimmies and shakes its tail to give you warning
Yet humans think they have the power to charm him

It doesn't knock on your door to inject its poison
Human presence in its domain just plainly annoys him
We track them down 'cause we want their venom
But we wouldn't need it if we'd just avoid them.

Snakes don't need our help to survive, don't forget
Their species has been here since day one and haven't gone yet
When you tread into their space, their cunning and wit
You deserve the agony you'll feel when you get bit

Looking Out Of My Window

I can see the seasons change
All kinds of trees, can't call them by name
Not only the seasons, i see
But any kind of weather whether sunny, rainy or windy

The leaves fall from the trees, it looks rather poetic
Seeing them being blown by the wind is hard to forget it
Looking out of my windows, i see the children playing
Running with their families, grandparents graying

That piece of glass in front of me is not really a pain
Though it's always called that again and again
Happily people go about their everyday lives with glee
And occasionally, I see a few looking in my window at me.

The Comedians

They arrive on the stage saying something funny
For that, they want us to pay them money
Their jokes sometimes funny most times not
But we want to laugh, for a short period our woes forgot.

Or is this a time for the comedian to let laughter hide his tear
So the need to laugh even for minute is for all of us here
Is the comedian making us laugh with their contrived banter
Or are we there cause we want to hear others' laughter

Laughing instead of crying at least for that moment
Funny or not that's the way we all want it
Laughter helps us cover up the wars, crimes in the newspaper
Women acting so badly, being bitchy, we have to hate her.

The comedian helps us focus on the junk we do
That is said in jest but many times true
Let laughter be the medicine you take to feel good
'cause the comedians sure wish you would.

Freedom is Not Free

Freedom is not free the price is too high
For you to feel free, lots of people had to die
Lots of souls set free with numerous challenges to tackle
Just so you and your children could be free of those shackles.

Instead of on your ankles, the chains are now on your mind
To keep your mind from growing, you anesthetize it with cocaine
Killing a child for his coat and shoes, cause you want'em
Don't want to get educated so that you coulda bought'em.

Stop kidding yourselves about how you'd fight for freedom
So that when you get it, your neighbors you want to beat'em
No, freedom comes with a price tag that should put you in check
But with your dumb ass, you haven't learned that yet

Why do you want to go to prison, and some of you that's where you'll stay

Until the electric chair or death by injection gets you out of the way
Sure this may be cruel and hard for you to digest or accept
But reality should set in to let you know, you're not free yet.

Would you appreciate freedom, if handed on a silver platter
No because you're gonna be a pain in the ass, it just don't matter.
I'm tired of looking over my shoulder wondering where you are
In my home taking something, or stealing my car.

Our forefathers must be ashamed of a lot of you
They wouldn't have fought so hard if they knew
That this privilege for which they fought and died
Would be abused, they might not have tried

Incarceration is voluntary, slavery is not
You'd rather kill somebody than pay for what you got.
Robbing and killing just like a goddamn fool
Do anything rather than taking your dumb ass to school.

Being in jail is worse that slavery could ever be
Do you crave incarceration 'cause you're afraid to be free.
Freedom is not a joke and shouldn't be taken for granted
The price of freedom is not dollar store priced, it's too gigantic.
Why these words are littered with words that are profane

Because said any other way seems you just don't understand
On this planet, all of us can happily exist
If only you would take time to appreciate this

Freedom is not free – not now not ever.

Without Inhibition

Uptight, scornful, judgmental and afraid
Trying to stay prim and proper when you want to get laid.
Fantasizing about love wanting it to come to fruition
To be able to make love with passion and without inhibition.

Fondling those ears, kissing those eyes
Touching being close without any surprises
Rubbing, hugging defying tradition
Making love without inhibition..

My ability to love under any condition
Is something I can't do without inhibition.

Smiling

Smiles – reassuring, bright and cheerful
Turns inside out into something fearful.
Even though you smile, you can't see its affect
It may be menacing or one you can't forget

The intent of the smile may put you at ease
A grin on your face so it depends on what you believe
Is that smile of approval, something you crave
Or is it as fake as the royal wave?

You're behind your smile so you can't see
What kind of expression you meant for me
Your smile of acceptance might need to be amended
'cause what i see, you may not have intended

You think you know peace and you do to some degree
How a smile is relative to what you perceive.
So when you smile make sure that it's true
'cause the world does not always smile with you.

Just for a Minute

Just for a second in a day
I want the world to turn my way
Just for a minute
I'd like to see a crystal ball with my future in it.

In a hour, my wish is this that I could spend a dime I wouldn't miss.
One day without confusion, chaos
In a world pretending to want peace at all cost.
A year has gone by, it seemed infinite
Despite the craziness, I've enjoyed my life if just for a minute.

Never Loved

Shame to say, proud to boast
Telling you, not seriously, that I love you the most

So many in love but for the wrong reasons
Taking abuse from others season after season
I never fell in love 'cause falling brings pain
I never wanted to hide teardrops in the rain.

Men and women in love as good as it gets
Until you realize you do it all just for sex,

Sex you don't have to earn, just go home
To find that special someone and not be alone
The world might be better off if you n ever loved
But concentrated on having sex and let be done.

In the rain

Warm, summer day, thunderstorm
So hot, even the rain is warm
But when it caresses your bare feet
It's a great feeling just can't be beat.

When the rain falls it makes you frown as it beats you
Don't know if its going up or coming down, it's true
When the rain falls and becomes more than the earth can drink
Rain becomes flooding faster than you can think

The rain disguises itself and fools you into thinking
You're dazed and confused like a drunk been drinking

One minute gentle, then its outraged, a monsoon
All your memories washed away, you're doomed
Hurricanes, raging winds mother nature irate
Your belongings have been moved to another state.

Gentle is the rain? Believe it if you will
Trust in it not until the raindrops are still.

Coulda Been

Don't you hat yourself from beginning to end
When you think about what you could have been
You coulda been anything or anybody, if you'd tried
You might have lived forever, if you hadn't died.

'cuz years ago, you coulda been a hero
Or spent your life on a beach as a zero.
You coulda been paying attention to your life
Instead of thinking about being someone's wife
Yeah I think about what I coulda been
But I realize I'm happy with the skin I'm in.

What I coulda been doesn't mean a lot
'cause I'm content with what I've got.

When Angels Cry

When all seems lost reality you defy
When teardrops fall is when angels cry
Teardrops come as a fitting disguise
For the moisture falling from your eyes
Angels cry because of the harm
You do to yourself doing what's wrong

Angels want us to live happy and free
They roam the earth making a way for you and me

Make contentment your goal
And watch happiness unfold
Such a great way you cannot deny
Keep the angels, they won't have to cry.

Don't Stop the Music

Don't stop the music
'cause if you do
You'll see how much life has affected you

You love music whether jazz or the blues
Country and western, classical and opera too
Swaying with the beat on the mighty drum
Tapping your feet waiting for that feeling to come

The harmonica crying out a soothing tune
The sound of the saxophone taking you to the moon

Don't stop the music keep it in your soul and inspire
Have life deliver resounding tones that unfold to rekindle a fire.
That you thought might have gone out lays dormant inside
Don't stop the music, love it, use, feel it and don't forget
That you've just started to live it.

Frustration

Too many medications
To handle any situation
That bring complications
Resulting in shear frustration

Noise levels too extreme
Makes you want to scream
Noting is as it seems
Need sanity to be redeemed

Frustration over little things
That grow incredibly big
Seeing a huge tree when it's only a twig
Frustration in being somewhere
When you want to be any place exotic
Feeling so good before, but now you forgot it.

Complications
Situations
Frustration